W9-CMH-335

All About Plants

All About

Roots

Claire Throp

Heinemann
LIBRARY

Chicago, Illinois

Edited by Claire Throp and Brynn Baker

Designed by Peggie Carley

Picture research by Ruth Blair

Production by Victoria Fitzgerald

Originated by Capstone Global Library Ltd

Printed in the United States of America in North Mankato, Minnesota

012015
008718RP

Library of Congress Cataloging-in-Publication Data

ISBN 978-1-4846-0508-0 (hardcover)

ISBN 978-1-4846-0514-1 (ebook PDF)

Acknowledgments

We would like to thank the following for permission to reproduce photographs:

Corbis: Eye Ubiquitous/Michael Peuckert, 18; Getty Images: a.collectionRF/Yoshiharu Nuga, 20; Shutterstock: Adisorn Chaisan, 12, Anake Seenadee, 14, branislavpudar, 10, Christopher Elwell, 4, Denis and Yulia Pogostins, back cover, 17, 21, 23 (middle), Filipe B. Varela, 5, leungchopan, cover, Maljalen, 22, Maximus Art, 9, Olgysha, 13, Pavelk, 15, Peshkova, 6, Sergiy Bykhunenko, 16, 23 (top), siambizkit, 19, Sunny Forest, 7, Surakit, 11, winnond, 8, 23 (bottom)

We would like to thank Michael Bright for his invaluable help in the preparation of this book.

Every effort has been made to contact copyright holders of material reproduced in this book. Any omissions will be rectified in subsequent printings if notice is given to the publisher.

Contents

What Are Plants?

Plants are living things.

flower

stem

leaf

root

seed

Plants have
many parts.

What Do Plants Need to Grow?

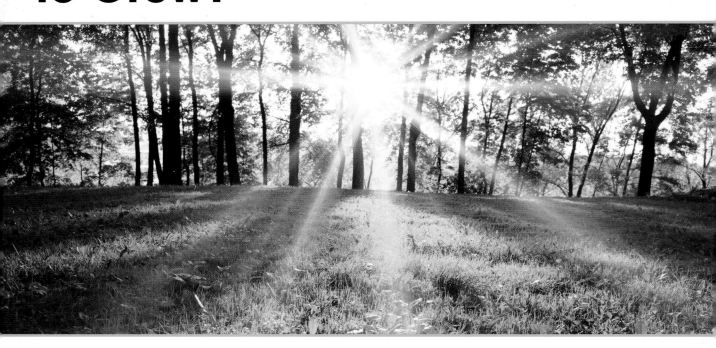

Plants need sunlight and air to grow.

Plants need water to grow.

What Are Roots?

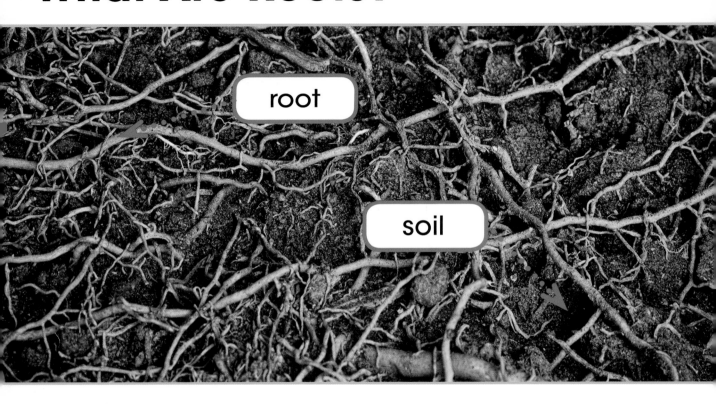

root

soil

Roots are one part of a plant.
Roots hold plants in the **soil**.

Roots take in water from the ground
to help the plant grow.

Where Do Roots Grow?

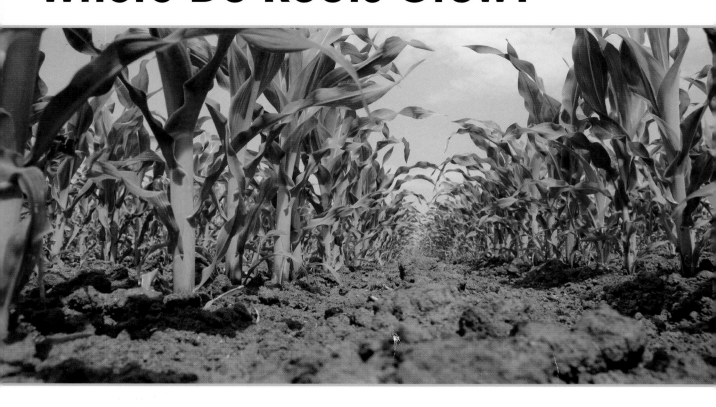

Most roots grow underground.
We cannot see them.

Some roots grow aboveground.

Some roots grow in the air.

Some roots grow into other plants.

Types of Roots

Young plants have small roots.

Old plants have big roots.

Some roots are **hairy**.

Some roots are **smooth**.

Some roots grow straight down.

Some roots spread out.

Roots as Food

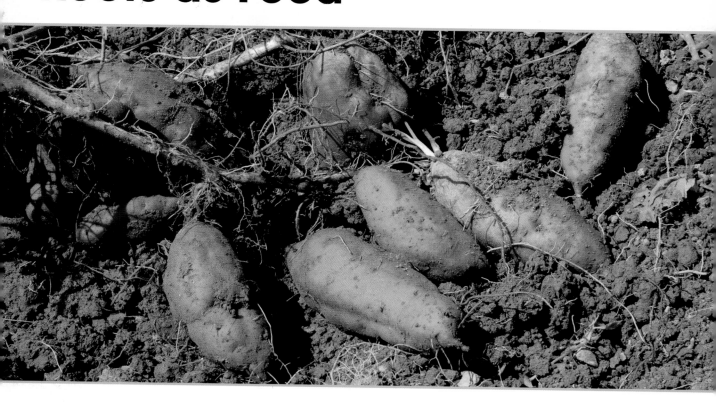

People like to eat some roots.
Sweet potatoes are roots.

Carrots are roots too.

Plants Need Roots

Water moves through roots into the plant. Roots help the plant to grow.

Picture Glossary

 hairy covered in smaller, hair-like roots

 smooth free from rough or hairy roots

 soil top layer of earth where plants grow

Index

Notes for Parents and Teachers
Before Reading

Show children the roots of a plant. Ask them what they know about plant roots.
Do they think all roots are the same?

After Reading

- Ask children if they can name some roots that we eat. Explain that
  some things we eat are stems rather than roots, but still grow under
  the ground. (potatoes)

- See if children can draw and label a whole plant without returning to
  the picture on page 5.

- Roots cannot always be seen, yet they are a very important part of a plant.
  Have children write two facts that support the following opinion: Roots are
  the most important part of a plant.